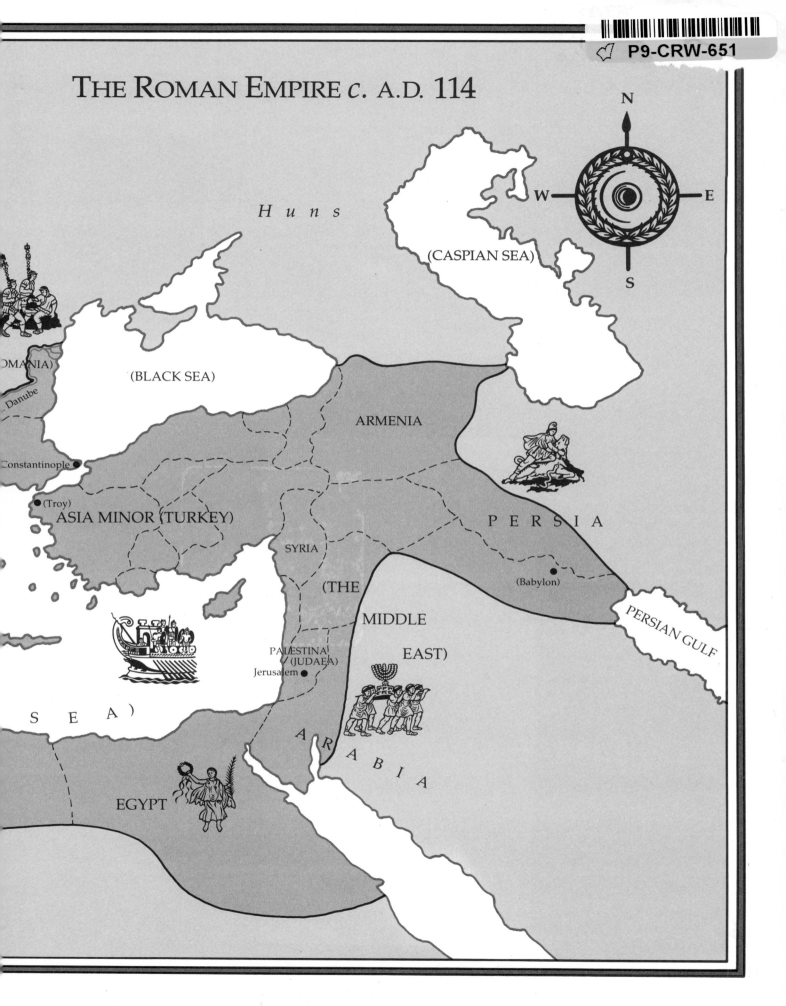

THE ROMAN EMPIRE c. A.D. 114

N
W · E
S

Huns

(CASPIAN SEA)

(OMANIA)

. Danube

(BLACK SEA)

Constantinople •

ARMENIA

• (Troy)

ASIA MINOR (TURKEY)

P E R S I A

SYRIA

(THE

(Babylon) •

MIDDLE

PERSIAN GULF

PALESTINA
(JUDAEA)

EAST)

Jerusalem •

A
R
A
B
I
A

S E A)

EGYPT

CLASSICAL
ROME

LIVING HISTORY

CLASSICAL
ROME

JOHN D. CLARE, Editor

GULLIVER BOOKS
HARCOURT BRACE JOVANOVICH, PUBLISHERS
SAN DIEGO NEW YORK LONDON

Copyright © 1993, 1992 by Random House UK Limited

First published in Great Britain by The Bodley Head Children's Books, an imprint of Random House UK Ltd

First U.S. edition 1993

Created by Roxby Paintbox Co. Ltd

Library of Congress Cataloging-in-Publication Data
Classical Rome/John D. Clare, editor.
p.   cm. — (Living history)
"Gulliver books."
Includes index.
ISBN 0-15-200513-7
1. Rome — Civilization — Juvenile literature.   I. Clare, John
D., 1952–   .   II. Series: Living history (San Diego, Calif.).
DG77.R6725   1993
937′.06 — dc20   92-30502

Director of Photography   Tymn Lyntell
Photography   Charles Best
Designer   Dalia Hartman
Production Manager   Fiona Nicholson
Typesetting   Thompson Type, San Diego, California
Reproduction   Columbia Offset Ltd
                                  Trademasters Ltd

Printed in Hong Kong

A B C D E

ACKNOWLEDGMENTS

Casting: Baba's Crew. **Costume designer:** Val Metheringham with Angie Woodcock, Ita Murray. **Makeup:** Pam Foster with Alex Vogel, Emma Scott, Michelle Bayliss, Nikita Rae. **Props:** Cluny South, Marissa Rossi with Eleanor Enghe. **Sets:** Tom Overton, Jim Dyson, Haydn Buckingham-Jones at UpSet. **Map and timeline:** John Laing. **Map and timeline illustrations:** David Wire.

Additional photographs: Ancient Art & Architecture Collection, p. 14 (center), p. 16 (bottom), p. 39, p. 44 (top), p. 53 (top); The Austrian National Library Picture Archive, pp. 50–51 (main picture); C. M. Dixon, front jacket background, p. 14 (bottom), p. 20 (top, center, bottom), p. 30 (top), p. 46 (top, bottom), p. 50 (top), p. 62 (bottom), p. 63; Fishbourne Roman Palace, p. 59 (top); The Gateway (Tyne and Wear Museums), Arbeia Roman Fort, South Shields, pp. 60–61; Sonia Halliday, p. 7, p. 16 (center), pp. 16–17 (main picture), p. 44 (center, bottom), pp. 48–49 (main picture), pp. 58–59 (main picture background), p. 62 (top); Museum of London, p. 37 (bottom).

Contents

The World of Rome

If the world were divided now as it was in A.D. 114, you could travel from Scotland to the Sahara, or from Spain to Syria, and still be within the Roman Empire. For your journey, you would need to know only one language and carry only one sort of money. You could admire the sophisticated Roman systems of public health, public baths, hospitals, postal service, fire fighting, civil service, and international trade and take in some of the most spectacular artistic and architectural wonders known to man — particularly if your travels brought you to the city of Rome itself.

Given the technology available, Romans of the classical era built what was perhaps the greatest empire of all time; Roman civilization has served as a model or a basis for much of Western culture. Roman engineers pioneered the use of concrete, glass windows, the dome, central heating, and apartment buildings. Roman roads, aqueducts, and buildings still survive. We still use the Roman alphabet, Roman numerals, and the Roman system of months. Latin, the official language of the Roman Empire, is the basis of many modern languages, including Italian, Spanish, French, and English.

THE BIRTH OF ROME

Modern archaeologists believe that Rome began as a collection of small wooden huts established about 1600 B.C. on a group of seven hills near the River Tiber in central Italy.

The Romans themselves imagined more romantic beginnings for their city. In his epic poem the *Aeneid*, the Roman poet Virgil claimed that his people were the descendants of a great warrior, a Trojan prince named Aeneas. Most Romans preferred another legend, told by the historian Livy, that suggested Rome was built in 753 B.C. by a soldier-farmer named Romulus. Romulus and his twin brother, Remus, were said to have been raised by a she-wolf — giving Rome a fierce, exciting beginning.

GROWING PAINS

As the city grew in strength, its leaders began to seek more territory. At first the Romans met with frequent defeats. After each setback, however, they returned to the struggle with even greater determination, and gradually they destroyed their enemies. During the fourth and third centuries B.C. they conquered most of Italy, including the south, where a number of Greek colonies were flourishing.

Contact with the Greeks, who had a more highly developed culture than the Romans, had a great effect on Rome. Roman literature, architecture, and religion were all greatly influenced by Greek traditions. Rich Romans bought educated Greek slaves from the conquered colonies to be their accountants and scribes, and during this period most teachers and doctors in Rome were Greek.

In 264 B.C., Rome went to war with the city of Carthage, the capital of a great empire on the north coast of Africa. This war lasted 120 years. The Romans suffered a series of disastrous defeats, but they also captured large areas of north Africa and Spain. Finally, in 146 B.C., they captured and destroyed Carthage itself, plowing salt into the fields around the city so nothing could grow there.

During the second century B.C. the Romans also overcame Greece and Asia Minor (modern Turkey). Some of Rome's new possessions were called "allies" or "clients" — here the Roman armies had not met resistance, and as a reward they allowed local rulers to stay in power as long as they paid taxes to Rome. Areas that resisted and were conquered, however, were divided into provinces and ruled by Roman governors.

SOCIETY AND GOVERNMENT IN THE REPUBLIC

The most basic Roman social group was the family. The *paterfamilias*, the oldest male, controlled the entire family, including his children and grandchildren.

Roman society was also divided into several classes. Many of the leading families — slightly less than 5 percent of the population — were known as patricians, or nobles; they held this rank by right of birth. Every freeman who was not a patrician was a plebeian. Some plebeians, such as bankers, factory owners, and merchants, were even richer than some patricians. Other plebeians were farmers, shopkeepers, laborers, or fortune-tellers. Although the nobles despised trade as "degrading and vulgar," the vast numbers of craftsmen and traders throughout Roman territory, no matter how poor, were still Roman citizens and had the right to vote in elections. Freemen (who had been born free) counted themselves better than freedmen (former slaves who had been freed). Women, however highborn, were not citizens, and they had few legal rights. They were dependent on their fathers or husbands and were not allowed to vote. Slaves, who were dependent on their masters, also had no vote.

The freemen of Rome believed they had the right and the duty to run their own government. At one time the Romans were led by a king, but in 509 B.C. they expelled the last one and established a republic that was led by two officials known as consuls, who were advised by a senate. Consuls, who also served as generals in times of war, were elected each year. When their period of office was over, they became life members of the Senate. Some senators were elected, but most were appointed by a consul. The senators were not paid but most had large estates and great wealth. During national emergencies such as famine or war the consuls might appoint a dictator, who would serve for up to six months. The dictator had absolute power and was expected to do whatever it took to restore order. In normal times, the Senate ran the country's government. The senators helped to regulate spending of public finances; they also regulated religion, declared war, and ratified peace treaties.

A bright young man from a rich family might serve in the army until his late twenties, when he might run for election as a *quaestor*. If elected, he gained entry to the Senate. Later, he might become an *aedile* (in charge of police work, public health, or public games), or a tribune (elected to safeguard the rights of the plebeians). In his late thirties he could campaign to be a *praetor* (judge and general) or one of the two consuls. Afterward, he might convince the Senate to appoint him as a provincial governor.

Left: *Rich Romans enjoy a boar hunt.*

7

The Roman Army

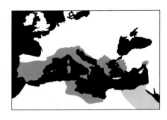

For a thousand years — from the fifth century B.C. to the fifth century A.D. — the Romans were continually at war. Their army became the most efficient in the world.

In the second century B.C., the army was made up of about 20,000 men. At the beginning of each year, the two consuls called all the landowning citizens between the ages of 17 and 46 to the Capitoline Hill in Rome, where the military tribunes chose the strongest men for the army. The men did not serve full-time but were called up when needed for a specific campaign.

The soldiers were divided into four legions. Each legion was led by a *praetor*, helped by a *legatus* and 6 military tribunes. The basic unit was a group of men, or legionnaires, called a century; a century could contain as many as 200 or as few as 80 men. A professional soldier called a centu-

rion commanded each century. Later, each century was divided into *contubernia*, groups of 8 men who shared a tent, a mule, and a millstone.

In an age when most battles consisted of a single wild charge, after which one side or the other turned and fled, the greatest strength of the Roman soldiers was their discipline. Roman generals, said the Greek writer Polybius, wanted men "who will hold their ground when outnumbered and . . . die at their posts." The soldiers fought in a series of lines, about 4 feet (1.2 meters) apart. First they threw their *pila* (javelins). Then they drew their swords, protecting themselves with their shields. As the men in the front line fell, those from the line behind stepped into their places.

After a battle, any company that had retreated was decimated — meaning that every tenth man was taken out and beaten to death with wooden clubs. Brave soldiers, on the other hand, were rewarded. As a result, Polybius warned, "It is inevitable that the outcome of every war the Romans fight is brilliantly successful."

As the Republic expanded, so did the need for soldiers. New legions were created, and in 107 B.C. the consul Gaius Marius realized that Rome needed a professional, permanent army. He allowed men without land to join the army as a career. By the first century A.D. soldiers were signing up for 16 to 20 years. At the end of their service they were given land for a farm. When not fighting or training, these soldiers were employed to build roads, bridges, and aqueducts.

Roman soldiers practice their fighting skills.
Left: *A senator and officers of the Roman army in the first century A.D. From left to right: a* signifer *carrying the standard of a century, an* aquilifer *carrying the eagle of the legion, a* signifer *carrying a* vexillum *(flag), a centurion, and a* cornicen *(horn blower).*
Above left: *The map shows Roman lands around 100 B.C.*

The Death of the Republic

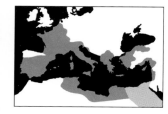

In the first century B.C., the Republic began to experience internal conflict. Politicians were corrupt, and by 44 B.C. there were more than 1,000 senators, all with large numbers of supporters (called clients) who relied on them for money and favors.

The Senate began to lose control of the people. Italian cities rebelled. In Rome, two senators — Marius and Cornelius Sulla — struggled for power. Both men were army generals, and in 87 B.C. Marius's men marched through the streets killing anybody he pointed to. Four years later Sulla entered Rome, drew up lists of Marius's supporters, and set out to slaughter them. Hundreds of citizens were killed.

In 73 B.C. a slave revolt began, led by a

gladiator (a slave who fought other slaves or animals in an arena) named Spartacus, who trained over 70,000 men to fight as an army. Spartacus initially intended to return these men to their homes in Europe, but his army's raids for food caused the Romans to send eight legions to fight them. After three years, the slaves were defeated; 6,000 slaves were crucified and left to rot along the Appian Way, the main road from Rome to southern Italy.

In 49 B.C., Julius Caesar, a successful general who had recently conquered Gaul (France) and invaded Britain, led his forces back from Gaul to Italy and marched down to Rome. There he seized control of the government.

Since being named dictator in 48 B.C., Caesar has tried to keep the provinces under his own strict rule; many Romans fear that he plans to make himself king. On the ides of March in 44 B.C., a group of assassins, led by the senator Cassius, murder Caesar in the Senate. One of the men, Brutus, is Caesar's friend.
Left: *The map shows Roman territory in 44 B.C.*

Rivals for Power

After Caesar's death, his friend and ally Mark Antony eventually formed an alliance with the young general Octavian, Caesar's great-nephew and adopted son. They went to war against the assassins, finally gaining control of the Senate by murdering 300 senators. Brutus and Cassius fled with an army to Greece, and in Rome Julius Caesar was declared a god.

Octavian pursued and defeated Brutus. According to the historian Suetonius, he sent Brutus's head to Rome and left the rebels' bodies to rot in the fields of Greece. In despair, Cassius had his own shield bearer kill him.

After their victory Octavian and Antony divided the empire and ruled jointly, Octavian in western Europe and Antony in Egypt. In Rome, Octavian made friends with the Senate and became a consul. In Egypt, at that time the richest part of the Empire, Antony fell in love with and married the bewitching and ambitious queen, Cleopatra. We do not know what Cleopatra was really like, since the Roman historians hated her and gave reports biased against her, but it is probably true, as many reported, that she believed she was destined to rule the world.

As Octavian and Antony each saw their individual power growing, they became rivals. In 31 B.C. Octavian's navy destroyed Antony's forces at the Battle of Actium. Antony committed suicide by falling on his sword; Cleopatra was captured but later killed herself, using a poisonous snake.

Antony and Cleopatra prepare to present their children to the Egyptian people, in a spectacle designed to show their power. Their daughter (center) is dressed in the costume of Libya, their sons as the kings of Persia (right) and Greece (left). Cleopatra is dressed as the goddess Isis.

Octavian Augustus

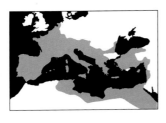

After defeating Antony and Cleopatra, Octavian secured his power over the Empire — by giving power away. In 27 B.C. he announced his plans to reform the Empire. The Senate, he said, would rule Italy and those parts of the Empire that were "peaceful and easy to govern." He offered to take the *imperium* (supreme power) in Egypt and in the provinces "that are restless and rebellious": Spain, Gaul, and Syria. Although he accepted the title "Augustus" (meaning "magnificent") he refused offers to become king. Thus Augustus, as Octavian was now known, showed shrewd statesmanship. He could claim first to have saved the Senate and the Republic from the rebels and now to be taking all the worst problems of government upon himself. The Senate, exhausted and unable to deal with growing economic and social difficulties, agreed to the plan.

The areas where there was a danger of rebellion, however, were also the areas where the army was stationed; Augustus had gained control of 22 of the 25 Roman legions. In addition, although there were no legions stationed in Italy, Augustus made

sure that he had armed forces in Rome. He enlarged his bodyguard — the Praetorian Guard — to 4,500 men and took control of the three units of soldiers who acted as the city police and the 7,000 *vigiles*, the soldiers who, among other duties, served in Rome's fire brigade. In all, Augustus had an intimidating 13,000 soldiers under his command in Rome alone.

Augustus was popular with patricians and plebeians alike. To revitalize the Empire's economy, he moved the treasury of Egypt to Rome. This enabled him to build up a huge following of clients; a hint from Augustus was usually enough to make sure that all the senators voted to approve laws he had proposed or to decide a court trial as

he wanted. He gave cash to every soldier and citizen, dismissed some landowners' debts, and out of his own funds paid unemployed men to work for the public. He provided Rome with grain, organized public entertainments, built many fine buildings in the city, and restored 82 temples.

Augustus concentrated on giving the Empire a good government. He managed to reduce many economic and social problems, such as crime, moral decay, and pessimism. He strengthened the army, introducing the idea of auxiliary forces: in each province, he enlisted native soldiers who were paid less than the legionnaires but were given Roman citizenship when they had finished their term of service. He attacked the barbarians in the north of Europe, reaching the frontiers of the River Danube and the River Rhine. At the same time, he disbanded many legions. Augustus's new administration kept all the appearances of the old Republic, but actually Augustus was an autocrat (sole ruler).

Before he died, in A.D. 14, at the age of 76, Augustus wrote the *Res Gestae* — an account of his reign and achievements, "whereby," he said, he "brought the whole world under the rule of the Roman people." He claimed he had "raised an army and set the Republic free." And indeed, Augustus is sometimes called the "second founder of Rome." His reign was the start of the *Pax Romana*, the "Roman peace."

Looking back on Augustus's reign in A.D. 38, the Egyptian Jew Philo praised him and claimed "the whole human race would have been destroyed, had it not been for one man, Augustus . . . who ended wars . . . set every city at liberty . . . civilized all the unfriendly, savage tribes . . . [and] safeguarded peace."

The historian Tacitus was less enthusiastic. Writing in about A.D. 90, he claimed that Augustus "tricked the army by giving them gifts, the common people by giving them cheap food, and everyone else by peace; then little by little he began to increase his powers, to steal the authority of the Senate, the magistrates, and the laws. . . . So the state had been changed, and the old, free Roman people no longer existed."

Augustus has the right to speak first in the Senate, so the senators always know how they have to vote.
Near left: *Livia Drusilla, Augustus's third wife and mother of his adopted son and heir, Tiberius.*
Far left: *The imperial family with members of the Senate.*
Far left above: *The map shows the extent of the Empire in A.D. 14.*

15

Rural Life

In Italy and throughout the Empire, the majority of the population lived in the countryside and worked on the land. Rich Romans gained their income from leasing small farms to plebeian tenants and preferred their country estates to the crowded towns. Roman writers praised rural values, comparing the "soft" city dwellers of Rome to the tough farmers.

The *pagani*, or "country folk," in Italy believed that every place had its numen (guardian spirit), which must not be offended; country life was full of religious rituals to please the spirits. Before a farmer could thin out a copse of trees, for example, he had to sacrifice a pig and say prayers.

Roman religion developed from the farmers' spirit worship, with certain spirits becoming more important than others. In the time of the Empire all Romans worshiped Jupiter, the weather spirit, who over the centuries had come to be considered the king of the gods. In the temple of Mars (the god of war, earlier known as the spirit of farming) priests still recited ancient farming prayers and performed a fertility dance, chanting and leaping into the air to symbolize the growth of the crops.

The Romans, whether city dwellers or *pagani*, were very superstitious. They believed there were a certain number of *dies nefasti* (unlucky days) in a year; on these days, no business was done and the Senate did not meet. The left side of anything was also unlucky; our word "sinister" is the Latin word for "left." To be safe, Augustus never put on his left shoe before his right.

Romans take care not to offend the gods. Hunters offer sacrifices to Diana, the goddess of hunting — "queen of the green forests, trackless glens, and murmuring streams" — before they set out.
Top left: *Each February 23, farmers honor Terminus (the god of boundary markers). At dawn, the boundary stone between two farms is crowned with a garland. The farmers build a fire and offer three handfuls of corn, some sliced honeycombs, and a sacrificial piglet.*
Center left: *Most farming is done by laborers using hand-tools. The soil of Italy is fertile and the climate is favorable, so crops grow well.*
Bottom left: *In Gaul farmers have invented a reaping machine.*

17

Gods and Religion

Early in their history, the Romans decided that the spirits they were already worshiping were the same as the gods of the Greeks. Rome's Jupiter, for example, was Greece's Zeus. Over the centuries the number of gods worshiped in Rome grew as the Romans adopted some deities of the countries they conquered and as more and more Roman emperors were declared to be gods after their death.

Roman deities had real personalities, character flaws, and emotions. Gods and goddesses often argued, and they fell in love — even with human beings. It was important for the Romans to know how these fickle gods felt, so they consulted prophets, augurs (who predicted the gods' wishes from the behavior of birds), and haruspices (who examined the livers of sacrificed animals for favorable omens). Most Romans would not travel, marry, or fight a battle if the sacred chickens were not eating.

When Augustus ruled, 66 religious festivals were held annually. The most important, the Saturnalia, honored Saturn, the god who was said to have brought prosperity to Rome. Many educated Romans no longer really believed in the official religion, but others argued that "this is the religion that made the whole world obey us."

To please the gods, these Romans conduct a sacrifice. A priest, his head covered with his toga, pours incense onto the altar while attendants bring wine, fruit, and a lamb. Romans believe that prayers are granted only if said in exactly the right way, so while one man reads the prayer out loud, another checks that he is doing it correctly, and a third plays a flute to drown out any other noises.

Romans do not attend the temples regularly; they worship the gods only when they want something. A young man might ask Venus, the goddess of love, to give him the opportunity to kiss his girlfriend. The generals might ask Jupiter or Mars for victory in a war. The Roman Army even offers sacrifices to their enemies' gods, trying to persuade them to support the Romans instead.

Trade and Traders

Throughout the Empire, everybody lived under Roman law and most people could speak Latin. As a result, trade flourished. Rome, said one Greek writer, was "a common market for the world."

Goods were usually transported by sea. It cost as much to carry grain 50 miles (80 kilometers) by road as it did to take it 1,250 miles (2,000 kilometers) by sea, and merchant ships could sail from Rome to Egypt in less than a fortnight.

Many of the imports that came into the city of Rome were tribute or taxes from the provinces. The port of Ostia, the harbor at the mouth of the River Tiber, 15 miles (25 kilometers) from Rome, was full of government officials checking deliveries, supervising loading, and paying crews. From Spain came wine, olive oil, honey, salt fish, wax, pitch, a red dye made from crushed beetles, black wool, and fine cloth. There were also wines from France, glassware and cloth from Syria, shoes from Greece, incense from Arabia, and marble from Africa and Asia. From beyond the Empire, the Romans imported Baltic amber, Babylonian

robes, gems from India, and silks from the Far East.

The most important trade was in grain; without large imports the Romans would have starved. Every year more than 400,000 tons of grain from Africa, Egypt, and Sicily passed through Ostia and the port of Puteoli, near Naples, on its way to Rome.

The merchants and tradesmen of Ostia and Puteoli formed *collegia* (social clubs), where they met each month to feast and to worship their genius (patron spirit).

Amphorae (large clay jars) that have contained olive oil cannot be reused because the oil soaks into the pottery and goes rancid, so the empty pots are smashed to be used as ballast on the ship's homeward journey.
Above top: *Scribes record the number of amphorae being unloaded from a merchant ship. The ship's rigging can be seen in the background.*
Above: *Cargoes unloaded at Ostia are put on barges and towed, sometimes by slaves, up the River Tiber to Rome.*
Left: *There is an extensive trade in fine glassware.*

The Streets of Rome

Although magnificent cities such as Alexandria, Athens, and Babylon flourished before Rome, it was the Romans who developed a true urban way of life, and Rome was the largest and most sophisticated city Europe had ever known.

More than a million people lived in Rome itself. Before large areas were destroyed by fire in A.D. 64, the city was a maze of busy, narrow streets. "However fast you hurry there's a huge crowd ahead and a mob behind, pushing and shoving," complained the writer Juvenal in the first century A.D. "The streets are filthy — our legs are plastered with mud — and you are sure to get a soldier's great hobnailed boot on your toe."

Julius Caesar tried to reduce congestion by ordering shopkeepers to move their wagons only at night, but builders' carts, rubbish carts, and religious vehicles were exempt — so the law made little difference. "There's nowhere a man can get any peace in Rome," wrote the poet Martial. "Shouting schoolmasters wake you up at the crack of dawn, at night it's the bakers, and all day long it's the coppersmiths with their hammers."

Graffiti scratched on walls proclaimed, "Don't pee here, the stinging nettles are tall"; "Iris only loves Successus because she feels sorry for him"; "65 sesterces [small silver coins] to anyone who brings back my copper pot." The smells from the hot-food sellers mingled with the stink of rubbish thrown into the road. Juvenal warned his readers: "Each open window may be a death trap — so hope and pray, you poor man, that the local housewife drops nothing worse on your head than a bucket of slops!"

A wealthy woman on a litter, a slave taking a boy home from school, a soldier, and others all pass a lamp shop.

The Forum

At the center of the city of Rome lay the Forum Romanum, an open space bustling with activity. It was a marketplace and a meeting place, the center of civic life. Other major Roman towns also had forums, but Rome's was the heart of the Empire; every milestone on every road in Italy recorded its distance from a marker set up in this forum.

Around the Forum Romanum ranged the law courts, the Senate House, and the offices of Rome's merchants and bankers. A sundial was centrally located, dividing the daylight into 12 equal "hours" of business. There were also a number of temples, including the Temple of Vesta, the goddess of the hearth (the focus of family life).

Each morning, the rich senators, wearing their purple-trimmed togas, wandered down to the Forum from their houses on the Palatine Hill; they might go to the Senate House or perhaps to the rostra — a public speakers' platform built from the *rostra* (prows) of captured enemy ships.

Eventually the Forum became so crowded that people had difficulty moving around in it. Augustus partially solved the problem by completing the Forum of Julius (started by Julius Caesar) and building the Forum of Augustus nearby, but central Rome remained crowded.

A senator (left), wearing a toga with a broad purple stripe, is going to the basilica (public building) to defend one of his clients in the law courts. Nearby, a boy who has reached the age of 16 receives his white toga virilis *(toga of manhood) from his father. Behind them, a woman reads her latest poems to a small group of friends and some of her husband's clients, and a funeral procession stops to hear a panegyric, a speech in praise of the dead person. Street vendors mingle with people who have met up to catch up with the latest gossip or to buy the handwritten newspaper, the* Acta Diurna *("Daily Events"). Tourists mill about, looking for the Tomb of Romulus.*

Women's Fortunes

The Romans believed that women were the weaker sex. Doctors thought that a woman's womb moved about inside her body (from her stomach to her legs) causing hysteria, fainting, and fits. Many families mourned when a girl was born; sometimes a baby girl would be left outside to die. Though they were allowed to go out on their own and sometimes to keep their own property after marriage, women generally had to obey their oldest male relative.

Marriages were arranged and an engaged couple seldom met before the wedding. A girl of 13 or 14 was ripe for marriage; before the ceremony, she had to renounce her childish toys. If a husband wanted control over his wife, he had to marry her *in manu*, in a special ceremony; otherwise she and her property remained her father's, even while she lived with her husband. "Hard work, lack of sleep, hands rough from working wool" — these, according to Juvenal, were the signs of a good wife, wealthy or poor.

Gradually, the position of women improved. Under Augustus, women got tax reductions for having children; women with three children got to wear special garments and were granted freedom from their husbands. A few educated women became teachers and doctors. Some, such as Eumachia, who owned a brickyard in Pompeii, ran successful businesses. Wealthy women discussed poetry and law and influenced politics through their husbands.

A rich Roman lady is dressed by her slaves. She is using a facial mask made of bread and cream; she puts in false teeth (imported from Germany), sucks sweets to freshen her breath, plucks her eyebrows, wears jewelry and false beauty spots, and uses powder, rouge, and perfume.
Above: *She wears a* **stola** *(dress) and* **palla** *(cloak).*
Below: *Her husband wears a toga.*

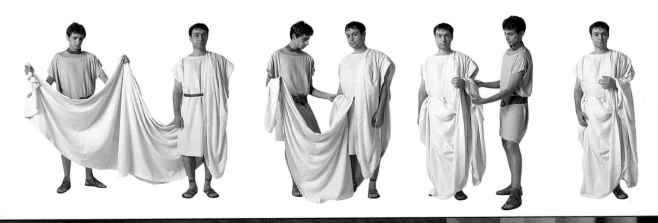

Morning Callers

The richest Romans lived in palatial mansions decorated with mosaics, wall paintings, and intricately patterned marble floors. Their elegant furniture was made of imported ivory, bronze, and fine wood.

In such a household, the *paterfamilias*, the oldest male, rose, washed, and shaved before dawn (unlike most citizens, wealthy Romans could afford private baths and running water in their homes). He and his wife would pray for the family and the emperor at the *lararium* (household shrine). The wet nurse fed the baby. Sometimes, but not always, the family breakfasted on bread and cheese. Boys, accompanied by a slave, left for school early, while it was still dark, perhaps buying something to eat from the baker's on the way. Girls might fix their hair and play quietly with a pet monkey while waiting for their Greek tutor to arrive.

A rich Roman would then open his doors

to a number of callers — his clients. These poor men depended on the six sesterces a day (or its equivalent in bread) he gave them. In return, they visited their patron every day, provided an escort for him in the street, accompanied him to the baths, and swelled the audience when he gave a speech or a public reading of his poetry.

Having greeted these callers, the *pater-familias* might visit his own patron, or he might hurry to the law courts, or perhaps to the Senate. Later in the morning, he would deal with business matters. At mid-day — after, in summer, perhaps seven or eight hours' work — he would have a light lunch of bread, cheese, olives, figs, and nuts, followed by a siesta.

These clients have hurried across Rome to say "Good morning, my Lord," to their patron. They are divided into two rows: "First-class" friends stand in front of the general public. The patron (left) ignores most of them and slips out with a slave, to salute his own patron before heading over to the Forum.

"Festina lente!" ("Take it easy!") cries the parrot.

Insulae

A survey of Rome taken in A.D. 350 showed that there were only 1,782 private houses in the city. Most people lived in rented accommodations in one of 46,602 apartment buildings, called *insulae* ("islands"). A typical *insula* was up to seven

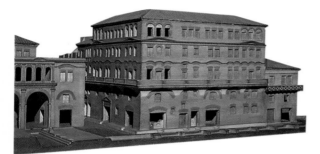

stories high, occupied a full block, and was bounded on all sides by streets, with shops on the ground floor.

In a few *insulae* rich and poor lived side by side, with a wealthy family paying 30,000 sesterces a year for a large penthouse. Most *insulae*, however, were not so grand; these were the homes of the poorer plebeians — the fruit sellers and fishmongers, butchers and bath attendants — who formed the bulk of Rome's population. In this layer of society, women could work alongside men or as midwives, dressmakers, or mime artists.

Rents in Rome were very expensive — 2,000 sesterces a year for even a tiny apartment — but most *insulae* were badly built and poorly maintained. In summer, the mud-and-wattle walls dried out, cracking and crumbling. Some tenements collapsed, killing hundreds of residents. Few of the plebeians' rooms had any heating apart from a charcoal brazier. The very poor had nothing to cook on; they ate cold food or bought snacks from taverns and hot-food shops. Water had to be carried up from the public fountains. A few *insulae* had a shared lavatory in the basement — otherwise people had to use public latrines.

This bread seller returns home to his wife, children, and elderly mother. "The simple life of the poor involves suffering every day — a pot with a broken handle, a fireplace without a fire, a beggar's rug, an old camp bed riddled with bed bugs," writes Martial.
Above left: *An insula in Ostia, the port of Rome, with a warehouse on the ground floor.*

Slaves

Romans often judged one another's importance by the number of their slaves (one senator had 4,116). Slavery was accepted as normal, and wealthy Romans liked to boast that they did nothing for themselves.

Most slaves were criminals or prisoners of war; Julius Caesar brought back one million men, women, and children as slaves from Gaul. All slaves' children were born into slavery. They were branded or wore a collar that bore the message "I have escaped. Send me back to my master."

Slavery was vital to the Empire's economy. The city government had its own slaves, who were used as builders and street sweepers. Slaves formed the work force of the factories and silver mines, where they were said to "pray for death, so great is their suffering." Farm work was also hard; city masters might threaten their slaves, "I'll send you to work on the farm!"

After Spartacus's revolt of 73 B.C., many Romans feared their slaves and often punished them brutally for small mistakes. One man used to throw his slaves into his fish-pond and watch as they were torn apart by huge lampreys. If one slave killed his master, all the slaves in the household were executed. Under the emperors, however, their status gradually improved; they were able to make legal complaints against their owners, and owners were forbidden to kill them without a magistrate's approval.

A master had the right to free his slaves and make them Roman citizens. Freedom might come as a reward for good service, or a slave could buy his own manumission; for example, an educated slave could borrow money from his master, buy a boy and train him, then sell him to the master at a profit. Sometimes a dying Roman set his slaves free in his will.

Above left: *A healthy man can be bought for 8,000 sesterces, although a pretty girl might cost 200,000, including tax. The sales contract states that they are "nonreturnable, except for epilepsy."*
Above right: *This intelligent young slave has saved the peculia (money gifts) his satisfied master has given him over the years and is now able to buy his freedom.*
Right, top to bottom: *Slaves do menial tasks and work as cooks, nurses, and masseurs in rich households. Educated slaves (often captured Greeks) are much in demand as doctors and accountants. Once it was proposed in the Senate to make all slaves wear special clothes, but the plan was dropped when someone pointed out that they would then see that they outnumbered their masters.*

The Baths

Although the houses of the wealthy had bathrooms, most Romans preferred the public baths, which usually admitted women from dawn to 1:00 P.M., men from 2:00 to 8:00 P.M. For a small fee any Roman could go to the bathhouse to wash, swim, jog, wrestle, meet friends, or conduct business. The statesman Seneca, who lived above a bathhouse, complained about the noise: "the man who likes to sing in the bath; men who jump into the water with an almighty splash; and then the cries of 'Cakes for sale' and 'Hot sausages.'" In the reign of Augustus there were about 170 bathhouses in Rome alone, and by A.D. 300 the number had risen to more than 800. The largest of these, the Baths of Diocletian, was completed in A.D. 305 and had space for 3,000 bathers.

Most baths had a number of different rooms. A bather would start in the *tepidarium* (warm-steam room) and move from there into the *calidarium* (hot-steam room). After perspiring in the steam, he or she took a warm bath, washing with a soap made from tallow and wood ash, then moved to the *frigidarium* (cold pool). Many baths also had a *laconicum* (extra-hot-steam room, for invalids), a gymnasium, gardens, a library reading room, and snack bars. Some baths were incredibly luxurious, their walls covered in mirrors and their pools lined with marble.

Some Romans thought the baths were a sign of a deterioration in the Roman character, and they looked back to the "good old days" when men washed once a week and smelled of the farm and the army.

In a small suburban bathhouse one bather is massaged while another has oiled himself and is scraping away the extra oil and dirt with a strigil.

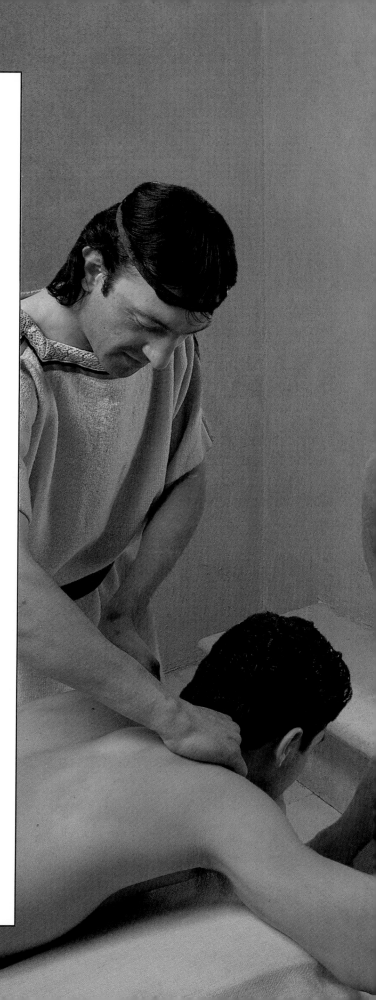

An Evening Meal

The *cena* (main meal of the day) usually took place in the evening. In wealthy households it was held in an upper room of the house called the *triclinium* after the couches on which the diners reclined. Men and women usually ate together, and the emperors invited both plebeians and patricians to their feasts — though the classes sat at separate tables.

Even for the wealthy, not every *cena* was a feast. Most meals were "humble little dinners" of fresh vegetables, bacon, beans, and sausage in semolina. Poor people had to make do, day after day, with cold food or porridge made from bread boiled in water, served in earthenware bowls.

But those who could afford it loved to eat to excess. Feasts began with an appetizer course — usually eggs, fish, and raw vegetables. Pork was the favorite meat; the main course might include teats from a sow's udder, or a lamb's womb stuffed with sausage meat. Desserts were usually fresh or dried fruit, seasoned with pepper to bring out the coolness of the fruit. When they began to feel full, guests sometimes made themselves vomit to make room for more food.

A good host provided entertainments such as singers, dancing girls, or comedi-

ans, in addition to keeping a lively conversation going. Politics was far too dangerous a topic of conversation; Romans discussed sports contests and such issues as whether smoking dried cow dung through a reed really cured tuberculosis. Drunkenness and bad behavior were common. All Romans were sensitive about their position in society. If a freedman felt he was being mocked, he might lose his temper: "I made my way successfully. So what are you staring at, you smelly goat?" In Pompeii, one host wrote his rules on the wall: "Be friendly and don't quarrel. If you can't do this, go home." At the end of the feast, less wealthy guests wrapped leftover food in their napkins to sell the next day.

These wealthy Romans recline on couches while they dine. Slaves stand by to offer more food and to clear up the mess as diners throw bones and scraps on the floor. **Below:** *In most houses affluent enough to have one, the kitchen is just a small room with a hearth and a sink. A wood or charcoal fire is lit on top of the hearth, and the food is grilled or boiled in bronze pots placed on a metal stand.*

After Augustus

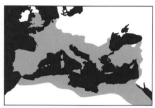

The accession of a new emperor was always troublesome. Though the emperor was entitled to name his successor, each possible heir had a faction of people working to get him on the throne. As a result, the imperial court was riddled with intrigue, and emperors and heirs constantly feared assassination.

TIBERIUS CLAUDIUS NERO,
A.D. 14–37

As Augustus lay dying in A.D. 14 he named his 55-year-old adopted son, the general Tiberius, as his successor. Tiberius continued Augustus's policies of peace and disguised autocracy. He refused the title of *imperator* (emperor), saying that he wanted senators to speak and vote freely and that he did not feel qualified to take over all of Augustus's responsibilities. For a number of years, wrote the historian Tacitus, Tiberius seemed to be a just and ideal ruler. He replenished the treasury and encouraged a return to traditional values and morals. However, numerous intrigues in his court made Tiberius uneasy, and he made it treason to say or write anything hostile about him. Consequently, none of the senators dared to reveal their true opinions. "This was a rotten, pitiful age of yes-men," commented Tacitus.

In private, Romans called their ruler Biberius Caldius Mero, a comic reference to his name, meaning "Drunk, Wine-drowned Boozer." He became notorious for cruelty and bursts of anger, perhaps sparked by his fears. When he died, people ran about joyfully, shouting: "Throw Tiberius in the Tiber!"

It was during Tiberius's reign, in A.D. 30, that a Jew named Joshua ben Joseph, known as Jesus the Christ, was put to death in Jerusalem by the city's Roman governor, Pontius Pilate.

GAIUS, A.D. 37–41

When Gaius, nicknamed Caligula after the tiny soldier's boots (*caligae*) he wore as a child, became emperor he threw a banquet for all the wealthiest Romans, gave every citizen three gold coins, and added a fifth day to the Saturnalia holiday. The historian Suetonius tells us that people thought their dreams had come true. To thank the gods, 160,000 animals were sacrificed in three months. "So much for Gaius the emperor," adds Suetonius. "The rest of my history must deal with Gaius the monster."

Gaius abandoned the policy of disguised power and ruled openly as an autocrat; he even claimed to be a god. According to Tiberius's will, Gaius was to have shared the throne with a cousin, but Gaius and the Senate declared his co-ruler too young to govern, and within a year the youth had been murdered. The Roman historians hated Gaius; they tell outrageous stories about how he made the legions collect seashells and proposed his favorite horse as a consul.

On January 24, A.D. 41, Gaius was murdered by his own Praetorian Guards. If Suetonius is to be trusted, people at first refused to believe he was dead, thinking it was a trick to discover what they would say. The story would have amused Gaius, who used to practice making faces in front of the mirror so that he could frighten people.

CLAUDIUS, A.D. 41–54

Claudius was tall and handsome, but Suetonius tells us that when Claudius was a child his mother called him a "monster" because he stammered and twitched. Suetonius also quotes a letter written by Augustus ordering that Claudius was not to be seen in public; Augustus feared people would laugh at him. So Claudius spent his youth studying history and writing books.

When he came to power, he was 50 years old; his studies had made him clever, and he was a popular emperor. During his reign the army conquered Britain (A.D. 43), and Claudius went in person to receive the surrender of the 11 British kings. Claudius ruled with the help of a council of ministers, including a secretary, a chancellor, and a financial adviser. He was the first emperor to invite citizens from the provinces to become senators.

Claudius was murdered in A.D. 54 by his fourth wife (his niece Agrippina), who wanted her son Nero to become emperor.

After Gaius's assassination, the Praetorian soldiers (below and left) search through the palace for a suitable successor. They discover Claudius hiding behind a curtain, and they proclaim him emperor.
Above left: *The map shows the extent of the Roman Empire at the time of Claudius's death.*

Christianity

B y the time of the Empire, few educated Romans believed in the old gods of the state religion, which was concerned mainly with formal rituals. Some people, wanting a personal religion, had begun to worship foreign deities, such as the Persian god Mithras and the Greek god Bacchus. Most Romans, however, were suspicious of these religions. The bacchants, who used wine in their worship, were accused of having drunken orgies; their religion was eventually forbidden. Christianity was considered just another of these "hideous and shameful" religions from the East, according to Tacitus.

Nero, Claudius's adopted son and successor, persecuted the Christians, accusing them of starting the Great Fire of Rome in A.D. 64. On Nero's orders, soldiers tied animal skins around some Christians, then attacked them with dogs who tore them apart. Others were coated with tar and crucified on stakes in Nero's garden; when it grew dark, they were set on fire to light Nero's parties. The emperor's cruelty, Tacitus wrote, merely made people feel sorry for the Christians.

Despite continued years of persecution, Christianity spread slowly and steadily. Eventually, 200 years after Nero's death, in the reign of the emperor Constantine (A.D. 306–337), it became the official religion of the Roman Empire.

The police raid a Christian meeting being held secretly in the catacombs, Rome's old underground burial chambers.

In their Eucharist (thankful) meals the Christians share bread and wine that they believe have been changed into the body and blood of Christ — consequently, they are accused of cannibalism. Because they worship only one god, they refuse to make sacrifices to the emperor, so they are also accused of treason. Most Christians share their possessions, and many are poor people and slaves, so it is said they are plotting against the rich.

Imperial Deeds and Misdeeds

If Tacitus and Suetonius are to be believed, Nero was an incompetent leader interested only in music, riding, and orgies. He performed in public as an actor and singer, wearing nothing but a dressing gown, slippers, and a scarf. During these appearances the doors of the theater were locked and soldiers patrolled the crowd, hitting those who were not cheering. For two years (A.D. 66 and 67) Nero toured Greece, "winning" prizes in the Olympics and other games for acting, singing, lute playing, and chariot racing—even though he fell out of his chariot. Nero was so pleased that he declared Greece would no longer have to pay tribute to Rome.

In Rome, however, old-fashioned Romans were angry that their emperor was acting in public and that he was mixing with Greeks. A string of plots were hatched against him, and the number of executions and forced suicides grew. Nero had both his mother and his wife murdered. One man was exiled because he was named Cassius, like one of Caesar's assassins.

Nero also began to lose control of the provinces of the Empire, perhaps because of slack government or because he was trying to reduce the powers of the provincial governors. There was a revolt in Britain, led by Boudicca, the queen of the Iceni tribe. The Jews of Palestina (Judaea) rebelled. The German legions grew mutinous.

Finally, in A.D. 68, Vindex, the governor of Gaul, revolted. He had no army, but he was supported by the governor of Spain, Sulpicius Galba. Nero panicked, and in June he tried to flee to Egypt. That night the Praetorian Guard deserted, after Galba's supporters bribed them. The Senate declared the emperor Nero a public enemy and sentenced him to be flogged to death. Nero committed suicide, stabbing himself in the throat and crying, "What a showman the world is losing!"

THE YEAR OF FOUR EMPERORS

A.D. 69 was the "year of four emperors," as different army commanders tried to seize

Nero, A.D. 54–68

Galba, A.D. 68–69

Otho, A.D. 69

power. First was Galba, who in A.D. 68 refused to make the traditional monetary gifts and alienated the Senate by choosing advisers who had not been senators. In January 69 he was assassinated in the Forum by the Praetorian Guard. Next came Otho, who committed suicide when his army was defeated by Vitellius, whom the German legions had declared emperor even before Galba's death. In December, Vitellius in turn was defeated and killed by legions loyal to Vespasian (who had had the prefect of Egypt declare him emperor on July 1). The civil war left the Empire in chaos. The Senate, which had supported all four claimants in turn, was a laughingstock.

Vespasian made the Empire into a military dictatorship. Proud of his plebeian origins, Vespasian modeled himself on Augustus. He rose before dawn, worked hard, and even tried to get up from his deathbed, saying, "An emperor should die on his feet." During his rule the wild parties and excesses of the previous reigns came to an end. Vespasian elevated numerous plebeians to the aristocracy and had them appointed to the Senate. He also revitalized Rome's economy, built or restored numerous public buildings, reorganized the army, and conquered new territory in Germany and northern Britain.

In A.D. 79 Vespasian fell ill with the fever that caused his death. "Oh dear, I think I'm turning into a god," he joked. He was succeeded by his son Titus, "the darling of the human race," whose declared ambition was to help someone every day; he continued his father's program of public works.

Titus's younger brother Domitian followed him. During the first ten years of Domitian's reign he seemed to govern well, but he became possibly the cruellest emperor of all. Though the arts flourished under his sponsorship of sculptors and writers, his harsh deeds alienated the Senate and the people, and in A.D. 96 he was murdered.

Rome's emperors mint coins with inscriptions and pictures (often of themselves) meant to impress the people of the Empire.

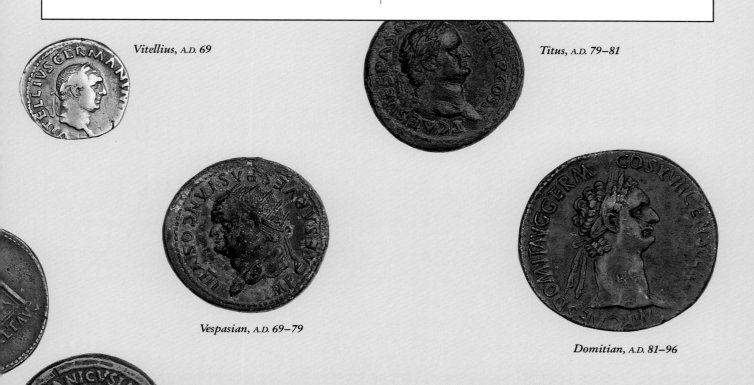

Vitellius, A.D. 69

Titus, A.D. 79–81

Vespasian, A.D. 69–79

Domitian, A.D. 81–96

Bread and Circuses

All the Roman emperors realized that to stay in power they had to keep the plebeians fed and entertained. They gave the *annona*, a monthly handout of free grain, to anyone who asked for it (there were riots if these supplies were late). And in urban areas they presented entertainments such as athletic competitions, chariot races, gladiator contests, and theatrical plays.

The emperors spared nothing to present a magnificent spectacle. At the Greatest Games, held in Rome by Nero, the emperor gave away food, money, slaves, houses, farms, and 1,000 birds each day. In one play the actor portraying Icarus actually tried to fly and crashed to his death, spattering the emperor with blood — the Romans relished such realism.

In the Greatest Games, Nero would not allow anyone to be killed intentionally, but this was not typical. Every year, thousands of criminals, slaves, and prisoners of war were made to be gladiators fighting one another or wild animals in Rome's arenas. Innumerable animals, particularly elephants, were slaughtered.

Chariots were raced at the Circus Maximus, Rome's grandest racetrack. Circular arenas called amphitheaters housed most other events — including mock naval battles, for which the bottom of an arena would be flooded with water. In A.D. 80, Titus opened the Colosseum, the greatest amphitheater of all; it could seat 50,000. To mark the occasion, games were held there for 100 days; 9,000 animals were killed.

At the games a secutor *(swordsman) has overcome a* retiarius *(net man), and the referee stops the fight. If the defeated man has fought well, the crowd will cheer and save his life. If he has fought badly, they will shout for him to die, and the official dressed as Charon (the boatman believed to ferry dead souls into the underworld) will club him to death. All gladiators, whatever weapons they use, are skilled fighters. Many survive long enough to buy their freedom. Some become famous stars and "the idols of the young girls."*

Top left: *A charioteer with one of his horses. Chariot races are wild and dangerous, and fans put curses on their favorites' opponents, asking demons to "torture and kill their horses . . . and crush the drivers."*

Center left: *Capturing animals for the games.*

Bottom left: *Loading ostriches onto a ship bound for Rome.*

The Building of Rome

According to the architect Vitruvius, who lived during Augustus's reign, "the majesty of the Empire is shown in the magnificence of its public buildings."

Augustus exaggerated when he said he "found Rome built of bricks and left her covered in marble," but he did contribute countless public works to the city. He built the Temple of Mars to dominate the Forum, and he gave the Temple of Jupiter seven tons of gold, plus jewels worth 50 million sesterces.

After the Great Fire of Rome in A.D. 64, Nero built on an even greater scale. His Golden House had walls covered with gold and jewels, a dining room with a revolving roof, and an entrance room with a statue of himself 120 feet (37 meters) high.

During the reign of Vespasian the building continued. The new emperor started the Colosseum, which required 400,000 tons of stone. Titus completed that project and continued Vespasian's work on the Arch of Titus, which depicts Titus defeating the Jewish Revolt in A.D. 73.

Rome, the "goddess of the earth," amazes visitors.
Above: *The Romans are outstanding engineers, using cranes to construct their great buildings.*
Right: *Slaves and craftsmen keep the elegant buildings in careful repair. Many buildings are covered in gold and marble; many interiors are decorated with mosaics made from small pieces of colored stone called* tesserae — *limestone for white and blue, brick or tile for red and purple, glass and ceramics for other colors.*
Below: *Visitors coming to Rome from southern Italy travel along the Appian Way (1) until they reach the Circus Maximus racetrack (2). Turning north, they go under the huge Aqua Claudia aqueduct (3) toward the Colosseum (4). Then they turn west along the Via Sacra, or Holy Road (5), past the Temple of Venus (6), and through the Arch of Titus (7) into the Forum Romanum (8). Open-mouthed, they look up toward the magnificent Temple of Jupiter (9) on the Capitoline Hill and feel that they are standing at the center of the world.*

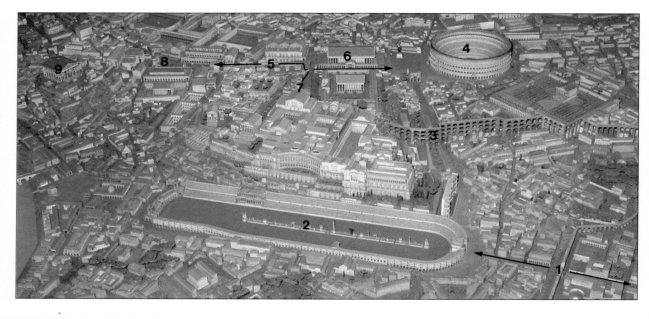

Aqueducts and Sewers

The Romans believed that polluted water and the "smell of excrement" caused disease. To keep people healthy and to provide water for fountains, they developed a system of aqueducts and sewers throughout the Empire.

The aqueduct system included siphons, tunnels, filter tanks, and arched bridges. By the first century A.D., nine aqueducts were carrying 222 million gallons (1 billion liters) of water a day from the hills into the city of Rome. The scale was vast: the Aqua Claudia was more than 40 miles (64 kilometers) long and used 600,000 tons of limestone in its construction.

Even more impressive, some claimed, were the city's seven underground sewers. Streams ran through tunnels large enough for a sailboat, washing the city's sewage into the Cloaca Maxima, the main sewer, and then on into the River Tiber.

Rome had a large number of public latrines. Each contained as many as 60 seats; here, in full view of everybody else, the

Romans sat and chatted. Everyone had a sponge (used like toilet paper today), which was rinsed in a channel of running water in the floor.

Introduction of Roman technology to the provinces has helped maintain the Empire's power there. In southern Gaul, the Pont du Gard, supported on arches, carries an aqueduct into Nemausis (Nîmes).
Right: *About a third of Rome's water goes through lead pipes to private houses. Householders pay for whatever water they use, so only the very rich can afford to let their water run freely. In Rome, as in all the Empire's cities, most water goes to temples, army barracks, and public cisterns and fountains, where most people obtain their water (in Rome there are 591 cisterns).*

Roman Roads

The Roman roads held the Empire together. They were its communication network, a key to its success and survival. They were so well constructed that they endured after the Empire had collapsed, and

legends grew up that they were the work of gnomes or giants.

The roads were used by a great variety of people: traders; mail couriers of the *cursus publicus* (a kind of pony express); government curators off to check the financial accounts of a province; proconsuls collecting taxes; Christian missionaries; athletes traveling from one race to another; thousands of people coming to Rome to see the sights or to put their cases before the emperor; and the legions off to quell unrest in the provinces.

Few residents of Rome enjoyed traveling, and most who left Rome became homesick. Traveling government officials could force local people to carry their baggage, but journeys were exhausting and people often died as a result of accidents or illnesses. Inns were smoky and dirty, and terrible firetraps. Still, most people preferred to sleep there than on the road, where thieves and other criminals made free.

The Peutinger Table is a medieval copy of a Roman map of the Empire's roads, giving distances between towns and the accommodations available. The top section shows the Balkans, the middle section shows Italy with Rome in the center, and Africa is at the bottom. More than 50,000 miles (80,450 kilometers) of roads cover the Empire at its greatest extent, in A.D. 114 (see map below).

The army builds roads. The surveyors plot a straight course from one landmark to the next. The engineers construct a strong base of logs and stones, then build up layers of different-sized stones, concrete, broken tiles, mud, and sand to create a well-drained, hard-wearing, smooth surface. In towns, roads such as this one in Ostia (left) are covered with large, smooth stones. At 100,000 sesterces per mile, the cost of road building is so enormous that it has to be paid by the emperors.

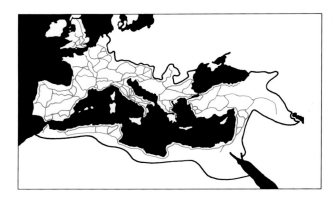

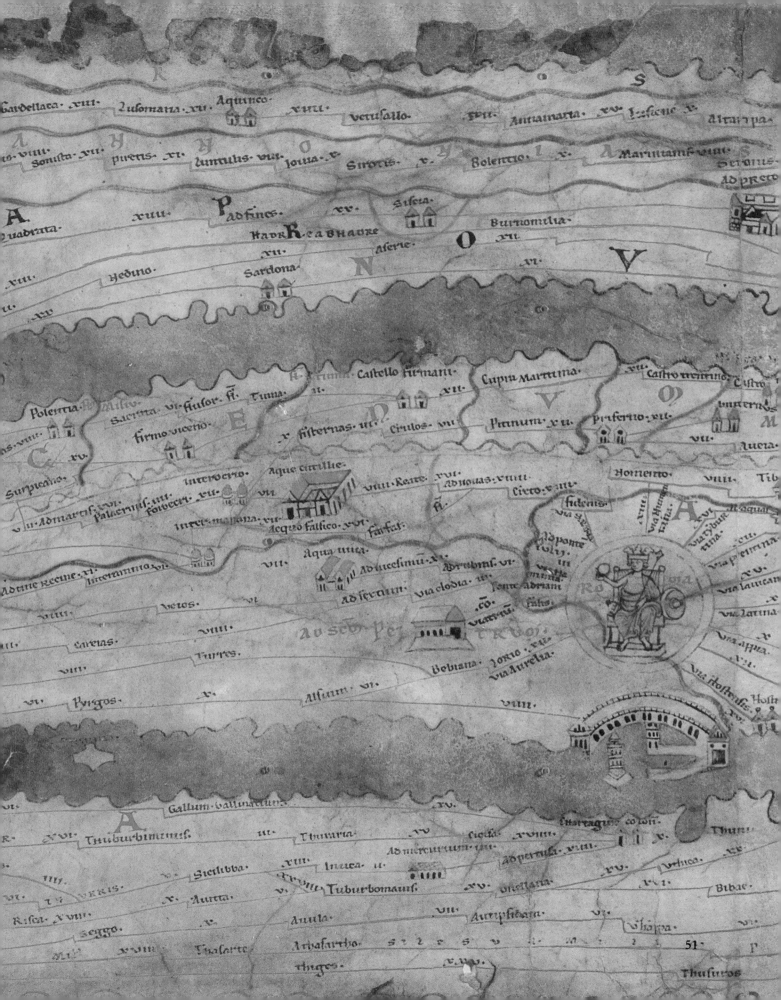

51

The Height of Empire

In A.D. 98, Trajan, the military commander of Upper Germany, came to power. Trajan was a Spaniard — the first emperor to come from a provincial family. During his reign (A.D. 98–117) the Roman Empire reached its greatest extent.

In A.D. 105 and 106, Trajan attacked Dacia, a crucial spot for maintaining power in Germany, and an invaluable route to the East. His army included perhaps 120,000 legionnaires and thousands of auxiliaries. He built a bridge over the River Danube, marched across the mountains, and stormed the Dacian capital.

Returning to Rome, Trajan organized 123 days of games to celebrate his victory. He built a new forum, including two libraries, more than 150 shops and offices, and Trajan's Column. He constructed a new aqueduct and a new bathhouse. To please the plebeians, he increased the *annona* and added a new benefit to support poor children.

In A.D. 114 Trajan invaded Armenia, and the next year he conquered the Persian Empire. But Trajan's huge empire proved impossible to hold together. In A.D. 116

there were rebellions in Persia, and Jews throughout the Empire rose in revolt. Trajan set out to return to Rome but died from a stroke on the way, in A.D. 117.

Trajan's soldiers attack and drive back Persian troops.
Above: A scene from the war against Dacia.

Exploiting the Provinces

For luxuries, the Romans depended on their wars of conquest and on the huge empire that they had built up. Soldiers were always on the lookout for valuable items to bring back from their campaigns. For instance, according to his doctor the emperor Trajan brought hundreds of tons of gold and silver, herds of horses, and 50,000 slaves back from his Dacian wars.

Once part of the Empire, provinces paid taxes; some taxes arrived as money, most as goods. In addition, each province had to support the legions and government officials stationed there. Quite often governors and tax collectors were not paid an official salary; they took as their wages any extra money they could squeeze from the inhabitants. "Spare a thought for the poor lo-

cals — you'll find they've already been bled dry," the poet Juvenal advised new governors, but generally becoming a governor was seen as a way to get rich quickly.

In North Africa and the Middle East, lions and elephants were wiped out to provide animals for Roman games. Forest clearing in North Africa reduced rainfall and destroyed the soil, which turned to desert. "The Romans have exhausted the land by their plunder. Robbery, butchery . . .

they create a wasteland and call it peace," the British chieftain Calgacus was said to have complained. It is interesting that these words were put into his mouth years after his death, by the Roman historian Tacitus. Perhaps the Romans felt guilty.

A centurion posted in Britain records the amount of grain a farmer is handing over as taxes. Britain supplies Rome with wheat, cattle, hunting dogs, bears, pearls, silver, lead, tin, salt, wool, and pottery.

Governing the Provinces

The emperor appointed a governor to rule each province of the Empire; the governor quelled riots and rebellions, and judged legal cases involving forgery, robbery, and rape, any of which might carry the death penalty. Wherever possible, the Romans used the people who had been in control before the conquest to look after local government matters such as roads, markets, temples, and the water supply. In some cases, the local ruler might even be allowed to continue reigning — with Roman guidance. The many peoples of the Empire could keep their own customs and religions, as long as they also worshiped the emperor: for Romans, this was not a matter of religion but a test of loyalty.

Romans believed that they were bringing civilization to a world of barbarians. "The Romans," claimed the Greek provincial writer Aristides, who was firmly convinced of the emperors' right to rule, "have . . . made life easier by supplying its needs and enforcing law and order. The whole world is as trim as a garden."

In practice, however, Roman rule was ruthless and often cruel. The Romans followed the principle of "divide and rule" — legionnaires recruited in one part of the Empire were sent to other provinces to keep order among people they despised. One governor in Asia executed 300 men in a single day and strolled among the corpses, exclaiming, "What a royal deed!"

The Romans encourage natives to develop towns following the Roman model, offering financial help to build temples and a forum in each one. Gradually the provincials adopt Roman manners and Roman clothes.

In very "backward" areas such as Britain and Numidia (where Trajan built a huge settlement at Thamugadi in A.D. 100), Romans establish "colonies" — cities of ex-soldiers — to serve as examples of civilized living for the local inhabitants.

Romanization

For the majority of peasants in the provinces, life under the Romans continued exactly as it always had. Throughout the Empire, however, wealthy provincials, encouraged by the conquerors, copied Roman ways. They went to the games, built bathhouses and theaters, and installed underfloor central heating. In Syria, Muttumbal, son of Auchusor, started calling himself Muttumbalius Auchusorius, learned Latin, and began to wear a toga. Africans built Roman-style villas and decorated them with paintings and mosaics. In Northumberland in England, a British farmer left his thatched Iron Age hut and moved with his family into a villa he had built next door.

In the later years of the Empire, thousands of provincials achieved Roman citizenship by buying it (in addition to the more traditional means of military or other distinguished service). Like Saint Paul in the Bible, they were able to say proudly, *"Civis Romanus sum"* ("I am a Roman citizen"). They could no longer be tortured to extract information, and if they were accused of a crime, they could go to Rome to appeal directly to the emperor to decide

their case. The richest provincials became senators and attended the Senate in Rome.

As the people of the Empire were "tempted to become peaceful," fewer and fewer men wanted to serve in the army; the government relied increasingly on men from the outlying provinces and beyond — Germans, Britons, and Syrians (who were often mutinous or disobedient).

The Roman villa system is introduced as the basis of agriculture in many provinces. A villa (right) is not just a manor house, but a complex of buildings. For the landowner there are living quarters with underfloor heating, wall paintings, colorful mosaics, and a private bathhouse. There may also be a farmhouse for the laborers, a

prison for the slaves, stables, cow sheds, storehouses, granaries with raised floors to keep out rats, and rooms for wine and olive presses.

The olive crop is gathered in December. Long sticks are used to beat the olives from the branches.

Decline and Fall

After Trajan's death Emperor Hadrian (A.D. 117–138) realized that if the Empire grew any larger it would become ungovernable. He concentrated instead on building forts and defending the frontiers.

Once the Empire stopped growing, however, it began to decline. Paralyzed by corruption and intrigue, the government became less and less effective. Between A.D. 138 and 361, 30 out of 42 emperors were murdered or killed in battle. Faced with the constant threat of assassination, many emperors either lived scandalously or became vicious tyrants. Taxes increased, family fortunes declined, and people had fewer children. Robbers and pirates disrupted trade routes. Perhaps most important, the northern frontier of the Empire was attacked by fierce and ruthless barbarian tribesmen.

In A.D. 330, in an attempt to keep control of the East, the emperor Constantine moved the capital of the Empire to Constantinople (Istanbul). In 364, Emperors Valentinian and Valens divided the Empire into two, thereafter to be ruled by separate emperors. In Constantinople the laws and culture of Rome were kept safe for more than a thousand years; Rome itself, however, was unable to resist the barbarian invaders. In A.D. 410 the Goths plundered the city, and in 476 the last emperor in Rome was deposed. Western Europe entered what some people call the Dark Ages, when classical law, learning, and life seemed to stagnate or disappear.

Roman soldiers guard one of the forts along Hadrian's Wall in Britain. Stretching 72 miles (116 kilometers) across the north of England, the wall has been built to try to keep out the Picts, barbarian tribesmen who live to the north.

How Do We Know?

There are many written sources about the Roman Empire available to historians. We can read the opinions of Roman politicians, generals, or travelers; we can read about the events of Roman history as they were seen by Roman historians such as Tacitus and Suetonius, or about everyday life in the short, witty descriptions of such writers as Juvenal and Martial.

These texts have to be used carefully. The Roman historians generally opposed the emperors, so it is difficult to establish what truth lies behind their hostile accounts. Tacitus openly admitted that he let his opinions influence his writing: "It is a historian's duty to praise the good things and to speak out against evil deeds and words." The writings of Juvenal and Martial are exciting, but the historian must remember that these men exaggerated life's problems to make people laugh.

RUINS AND REMAINS

The Romans were excellent engineers, and many of their buildings and monuments made of stone and concrete still stand. Aqueducts from the Empire supplied Rome with water into the 20th century. In Rome the tourist can visit the remains of the Forum Romanum, the Colosseum, and the Arch of Titus. The relief carvings on Trajan's Column have been a major source for historians of the Roman army and are one of the few sources we have for Trajan's Dacian wars. If you go to Nîmes, in France, you can still see the Pont du Gard aqueduct, visit a Roman amphitheater, or walk into a Roman temple (now called the Maison Carrée). At Timgad, in Algeria, (the Roman Thamugadi), you can see the well-preserved ruins of a complete Roman city. In the

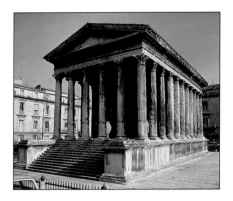

north of England, historians can walk along the remains of Hadrian's Wall and imagine they are Roman soldiers watching for Picts.

In the 19th century, the Italian archaeologist Giuseppe Fiorelli began excavating one of the most remarkable sites of all—the town of Pompeii, buried under a mountain of ash when Mount Vesuvius erupted. Everything was preserved exactly as it had been at the moment when life in Pompeii stopped, in the early afternoon of August 24, A.D. 79. On the ground floor of one *insula*, in the bar that belonged to Asel-

lina (her name is painted on the wall), excavators found water that was being heated in a kettle 18 centuries earlier. Where people were buried by the eruption, cavities were left as their bodies decayed. Fiorelli devised a method of pouring plaster into the holes to make casts of the bodies in the positions they were in at the moment of death: a girl hiding her face in her father's clothes; a family fleeing down the street, overcome by the ash and fumes — the children falling first, then the mother, and finally the father.

In addition to these and other archaeological sites and artifacts, there are thousands of inscriptions (telling us about the careers of the people they commemorate), as well as mosaics, wall paintings, and graffiti, all of which give us insight into the everyday lives of the Romans. Roman coins are so numerous that they are quite cheap to buy; they are important to the historian because the inscriptions and pictures on them were used as propaganda by the emperors and therefore reveal what the rulers wanted people to believe.

THE RENAISSANCE AND ROMAN CULTURE

Beginning in the second half of the 15th century, there was a renaissance (rebirth) of interest in Roman civilization, especially after 1453, when the Turks captured Constantinople and refugees took a large number of Latin documents back to western Europe. Years later, in Italy, Pope Clement XIV (1769–1774) founded the Vatican Museum and collected Roman remains. In England and France, architects copied the Roman style of building, developing what became known as the "classical style" (because it was considered to be

without equal). A study of Latin texts (called "classics") and a "grand tour" of Italy were an essential part of the education of wealthy young Europeans in the 18th century; many Americans also made the "grand tour" in the 19th century.

Between 1776 and 1788 a young Englishman, Edward Gibbon, published his epic book, *The Decline and Fall of the Roman Empire*. The book describes the Roman Empire sinking under the "slow and secret poison" of tyranny and decadence, until "the fierce giants of the north broke in and restored a manly spirit of freedom." Gibbon has influenced historians of the Roman Empire ever since.

THE PAST IN THE PRESENT

Roman civilization has survived in another, less obvious way, passed down through the ages in the traditions, institutions, attitudes, and even foods of the Western world. During the time of the Empire, a fish sauce called *garum* became popular all over Europe and even farther afield. In India it continued to be used until the 19th century, when British government officials rediscovered it and brought the recipe back to England, where it is now sold as Worcester sauce.

Over the years, a great deal has changed beyond recognition. Where Roman traditions still survive, they have often lost their original meanings. Newlywed husbands still carry their wives across the threshold, but no longer to demonstrate their control over the household. Despite the changes, however, Rome provided the foundation on which modern civilization was built. There is a little of the Roman in all of us.

At Pompeii, the plaster cast of a girl (near left) conveys the sadness of the disaster. Stepping stones in the street (far left, below) prevented feet from getting muddy. Far left, above: The Maison Carrée in Nîmes.

Index